How to Make Kombucha

Everything You Need to Know

How to Make Kombucha at Home, Most Delicious Kombucha Recipes, Simple Methods, Useful Tips, Common Mistakes, FAQ

By: Jason Goodfellow

Legal notice

Copyright © 2017 by Jason Goodfellow
All Rights Reserved.

No one is allowed to copy this book, or distribute again, or reproduce it, publish it, perform it, display it, modify it, or even create any type of any derivative works. No one is allowed to transmit, or also exploit any small part of this document.

And without any written permission from the publisher, except when using samples of quotations, you are not allowed to use this document for any commercial uses, but the use is only allowed by the law of copyrighting. If you have any permission requests, please feel free to write to the publisher.

The information contained in our book is provided for only informational purposes and shall never be construed as a form of medical advice or even instruction. Readers are advised to consult a licensed health care professional concerning all matters related to their health issues.

Table of contents

Book Description 1

Introduction 3

Chapter 1: History and Origins of Kombucha 5

Chapter 2: The Kombucha Culture and Fermentation ... 9

Chapter 3: Major Types of Fermentation 11

Chapter 4: Types and Variations of Kombucha Tea 14

Chapter 5: How to Grow Scoby 17

Chapter 6: Kombucha Equipments 19

Chapter 7: Benefits of Kombucha 23

Chapter 8: Delicious Kombucha Recipes 26

    Recipe 1: Kombucha with Ginger flavor 27

    Recipe 2: Kombucha Tea 30

    Recipe 3: Kombucha tea 32

    Recipe 4: Oregano Chamomile Kombucha 34

    Recipe 5: Pumpkin Kombucha 37

Recipe 6: Peach Kombucha 39

Recipe7: Carrot Kombucha 41

Recipe8: Mango Kombucha 43

Recipe 9: Strawberry Kombucha 46

Recipe 10: Cranberry Kombucha 48

Recipe 11: Kombucha with Fruits and Green Tea .50

Recipe 12: Blueberry Kombucha with Mint 52

Recipe 13: Kombucha Cocktail 54

Recipe 14: Cucumber Kombucha 56

Recipe 15: Blackberry Kombucha 58

Recipe 16: Apple Kombucha 60

Recipe 17: Beer Kombucha 62

Recipe 18: Kombucha Candies 64

Recipe 19: Kombucha Ketchup 66

Recipe 20: Kombucha Cookies 68

Recipe 21: Kombucha bread 70

Recipe 22: Kombucha Brownies 72

Recipe 23: Kombucha Carrot Cake 74

Recipe 24: Grapes Kombucha 77

Recipe 25: Kombucha Salad 79

Chapter 9: Kombucha Tips 81

Chapter 10: Common Kombucha Mistakes 86

Chapter 11: Diverse Kombucha Frequently Asked Questions 91

Conclusion 99

Book Description

WHY YOU SHOULD READ THIS BOOK?

The Chinese believe that kombucha can open our third eye. It's time we better understood how important kombucha is for health and the human body. While kombucha is known worldwide by its power in cleansing the body and the soul, many people still don't know what kombucha is. To enlighten people about what kombucha is, we are happy to share with you this book that will introduce you to the wonders of kombucha as we share our knowledge in this book. And in addition to giving you a clear and detailed explanation of what kombucha is, you will find information on the cultural level, too. Kombucha is indeed a Manchurian type of mushroom, which is based on a combination of fungi and bacteria that we may brew and drink as a high-quality, cleansing tea. It is generally known that kombucha is a drink which is fermented and then prepared by combining the sugar and the black tea. It is also said that kombucha plays a very important role in energizing and detoxifying physical as well as the spiritual health. So, if you are curious to know how you can make kombucha at home and how to use it in different succulent recipes, this book will make a perfect guide for you. You will be find out how to make kombucha your way to a healthy lifestyle. The recipes you will find in this book will introduce you to a variety of flavor combinations. This booklet will, in addition, allow you to learn the different types, brewing methods, common mistakes, and various FAQs that will make you addicted to drinking kombucha. This book will include many benefits of drinking kombucha, and you will even get an opportunity to learn its origins back in history and fascinating information about the various health benefits of kombucha. We can assure you that you won't taste anything better than your homemade kombucha drinks.

You will discover:

• Detailed information on how much of the kombucha drink you need to consume per day, and the content of alcohol in a kombucha drink.

• A wide variety kombucha drink recipes and even pieces of advice on how to master making kombucha in a short period of time

• How to make delicious cocktails from kombucha

• How to use kombucha to cleanse your body

• Ways to store your kombucha drinks

Get ready to get your kombucha brew on with its fragrant as well as fresh taste, and more!

Introduction

Some people call kombucha a Tea of Immortality or what is called Cha in the Chinese language. Kombucha refers, indeed, to the stomach treasure or the sea treasure; while some other people call it the sea mushroom, nowadays kombucha is known as hongchajun which signifies the red tea mushroom or the chameijun. But if you ask tens of people where kombucha came from, you will get no answers because most of them wouldn't even understand the word itself. Kombucha is a known beverage that is obtained from fermenting the sugar and the tea with a culture of bacteria. Some researchers call the kombucha scoby which refers to the "mother of mushroom". Kombucha is known for its refreshing taste that resembles that of champagne and apple cider. Kombucha is made of sugar and tea, but how about bacteria? Studies and researches have always focused on kombucha being a concoction of bacteria. Fans of kombucha tea believe that the well-known tea made of the kombucha mushroom provides us with a variety of perks both on the physical and the spiritual levels. However, the American heritage strongly suggests that kombucha refers to the Japanese heritage and it is a tea made of Kombu, which is a Japanese word that designates the tea that is fermented because of the thick film of gelatinous that looks like seaweed. In the Japanese language, kombucha designates kelp tea, which is a brownish drink made of the dried, then powdered kelp. Kombucha is classified as a probiotic and it is no secret that it is used in both Eastern and Western medicine for its incredible health benefits. Many medicinal cultures have praised kombucha for the great role it plays in metabolism and in improving the immune system. And as days go by, kombucha consumers are spreading worldwide and this is why we are offering you this book, with all the clear directions you need to know in order to make your own brewed kombucha drinks. This book reveals many secrets you didn't know about the uses of kombucha and brewing it. You will also find some of your favorite recipes with herbs, fruits and spices, and cocktails too. And even if you haven't yet tried making kombucha, stop waiting and learn how to mix this extremely healthy brew and include it in your daily everyday lifestyle. Not only beginners will like this book, but also very experienced brewers will feel curious to have a look at the recipes included in it. Experienced brewers will also like kombucha basic recipes with the innovative twists and the quick cooling method of kombucha brewed tea. So whether you are an expert in brewing kombucha or a new beginner, this simple and clear book will make a great addition to your library, or you can also choose it as a gift for your friends and for your family too. Not only does the book include simple and delicious kombucha recipes, but it also includes nice pictures that you will enjoy. In this book, you might find an answer to the question why kombucha is known as the elixir of our lives that cleanses the body of cancer.

Chapter 1: History and Origins of Kombucha

Researchers agree that any invention, creation or concept that is passed down from generation to generation and from one culture to another is worth studying. Kombucha is no exception and there must be a reason why it found its way to our modern culinary traditions. Indeed, the dependence on consuming kombucha stems from the rising awareness of people to get used to healthy drinks and food. Many of the traditional meals that make an indispensable part of our daily routines are characterized by possessing bioactive elements. Kombucha tea is also a functional ingredient that is produced by the function of fermentation. Kombucha tea has immensely spread and gained an unrivaled popularity in our recent days because of its health benefits and thanks to its therapeutic value. The invention of kombucha dates back to 220 BC and exactly to the Qin Dynasty under the reign of the Chinese Emperor called Qinshi Huangdi. Many stories and legends were associated with kombucha, and one of the most known tales originated thousands of years ago, in the District of Bohai Sea, not very far from Beijing. The legend started in a Bohai family that used to own a small grocery and that specialized in selling sundries. As the legend relates, there was an assistant who was rinsing a jar of honey when he sloshed a little quantity of that rinsed water into a crock that was filled with wine. The assistant didn't give any importance to what happened, but the story didn't end there, and after a few days, everyone started smelling a weird scent that was both sweet and sour. All the neighbors and the people became curious and eager to find out the source of the unknown aroma, but no matter how hard they tried, no one was able to reveal the secret of the strange scent. Even the owner of the shop tried to track the source of the aroma, but failed and the issue drove the man crazy. He decided to sell the stored wine. When the assistant of the shop opened the cover of the wine jar, he loudly screamed when he smelled the flavor that was coming of the jar. At that moment all the people who were passing by the shop rushed in to see what happened to the man, thinking that he was bitten by a snake. It was then when the shop assistant discovered a thick layer that resembled the white milk right on top of the crock and based on that smell, the first kombucha culture was developed; it was like treasure to them.

The owner of the shop decided to keep the wine and not sell it, but the shop assistant was curious to taste the thick layer of the milk and he forced himself to wait until the summer. However, when the weather turned out to be very hot during the summer, the shop assistant couldn't resist the thirst anymore and he tasted the nectar from the jar. With a dipper, the shop assistant drank from the crock without leaving even one drop of the drink. As people watched how the assistant was eagerly drinking, they asked him to give them the drink so that they could understand how the drink tasted. The assistant of the shop tried his best to remember what the drink was made of and from that instant, he started using the technique he used on another type of sweet vinegar. Thanks to the invention of the shop assistant, the business of the shopkeeper flourished and he was able to drink kombucha with the culture that was served with a dressing and he was known as the first expert in brewing kombucha. After the man's death, the secret of kombucha was spread and shared all around the globe. Maybe the main reason why kombucha was called the Sea Treasure was that it appeared in the District of Bohai.

The Chinese people were also very well-known for the use of kombucha in Chinese medicine because of their constant search for natural cures and remedies for their medical and health conditions. The Japanese launched their first studies to look into the origins of kombucha and according to Korean history a Korean doctor who was called Dr Kombu took kombucha with him to Japan as a gift for a Japanese Emperor known as Inyoko in the year 414 AD. And later on, the great warriors of Japan, called Samurai, carried with them kombucha in their ferocious battles and it gave them energy and power. Other people believed that kombucha originated from a fermented vinegary beverage that Genghis Khan used to fill his flasks with in his battles. It was also believed that Genghis Khan was the one who invented barbecuing.

And away from the Asian continent, kombucha found its way to Russia and to the European continent thanks to the business of silk and the road that connected Asia to Russia. And the exact history of brewing and drinking kombucha started in Russia and Ukraine by the end of the 19th century and the culture of kombucha was rather called čajnyj grib, which signifies the tea mushroom, and it even won a Nobel Prize. Kombucha became popular on the Russian continent and spread to Europe, and it was not until the Second World War that it started to be modified by the use of sugar tea. It was very difficult for poor families to brew kombucha because of the shortage and the high prices of sugar and red tea. Some people even considered it a privilege to consume kombucha. Thus, brewing kombucha faded away in the after math of the Second World War, but it appeared later in the Italian elite where it was spread again to Eastern Europe. During the previous few decades, the use of kombucha was revived in Australia and Europe as well as the United States. Kombucha names changed so much through history. From Russia, to Prussia and Poland; then Germany to Denmark; kombucha was later used in treating cancer, high pressure, some digestive disorders and even diabetes cases.

Chapter 2: The Kombucha Culture and Fermentation

We call a kombucha culture a scoby that resembles a pancake. It is characterized by its creamy color and it is used to brew the black tea. The kombucha culture keeps regenerating every time we brew it. Kombucha culture signifies a symbiotic culture made of yeasts and bacteria. It is generally known that kombucha culture is added to the sweetened green or black tea and it transforms an ordinary cup of tea into a cup full of vitamins, enzymes, and minerals.

Scoby, in etymology, is derived from an acronym that refers to the Symbiotic Colony of Yeast and Bacteria. The kombucha cultures are known as the mother of cultures and it is a mushroom, but not necessarily a fungi. A culture scientifically refers to what is called a zoogleat mat, while the scoby usually takes the shape of a container. The thickness of a scoby or culture differs based on the rate of acidity of the medium used in the period of the kombucha development. The yeast developed in kombucha can contain brettanomyces bruxellensis, saccharomyces cerevisiae, schizosaccharomyces pombe, andzygosaccharomyces bailii, candida stellata and torulaspora delbrueckii, or any other type of strain. However, the fermentation of kombucha varies from one culinary tradition to another and from one culture to the other. It is also the concentration of alcohol that helps in producing the acetic acid thanks to the presence of bacteria. You may also wonder how the process of fermentation takes place; it is all based on the active function of yeasts and bacteria. But some people may wonder what fermentation is and how it takes place.

Fermentation

Ever since human beings started living on earth, fermentation was always connected to them and their lifestyle. Fermented beverages appeared first in a few cultures; then it spread to different cultural traditions in diverse countries and continents. Studies have found that most of the vertebrate species are characterized by a hepatic enzyme functional system that it uses in order to metabolize alcohol. Scientists have always been interested in studying the different effects of a wide variety of beverages that ignite happiness and joy. Even primitive human beings and our first ancestors ate fermented fruits in huge quantities and since then, human kind has never stopped its evolution.

Chapter 3: Major Types of Fermentation

It is known worldwide that beer and wine are the main types of fermented drinks, but they are not the only fermented drinks; there are several other delicious and popular varieties. So let us have a closer look at the diverse types of fermented drinks that use a variety of interesting ingredients.

1. Dark Or Black Tea

Dark or black tea is originated from China and it is a type of tea that was fermented from the Chinese continent. In order to prepare dark tea, the leaves are rolled, then moistened and then we leave the tea aside to ferment for a period of time that can be a year or so. After the tea leaves ferment, we drink the fermented tea. The leaves of the black tea usually become black and then are used in making cakes. A very popular type of dark tea is derived from the Chinese province Yunnan.

The Chinese people use the dark tea in different types of ailments and for certain health conditions. In fact, when the tea is fermented, its flavor changes to be richer in texture and its taste becomes like the taste of dried dates.

2. Cider

Cider has always played a very important role in the America culinary traditions, especially in colonization. It was said that cider was a popular drink in New England because there were many apple orchards and fruits available for fermenting. During the year 1767, the consumption of cider exceeded 35 for each person; but its consumption declined later.

3. Basi

Basi is a great type of fermented drink because it resembles wine, however the difference is that Basi is made with sugar cane. There are various traditional methods as far as making Basi is concerned and it depends on the difference between regions. The mostly known conventional method of preparing Basi relies on boiling the sugar cane juice and combining it with the leaves of samak as well as with barks. The leaves are characterized by the high presence of Saccharomyces cerevisiae and wine yeast in it. After the stage of fermentation, the wine of the base keeps for about 6 to 11 months in earthen jars. You can find a base that can be aged more than 9 years and in general, the best types of Basi gains 1% of alcohol per year. Basi is characterized by its sour and sweet with a twist of bitterness.

4. Kimchi

Kimchi refers to a pickled and spicy product that originates from Korea and is made in various types and styles. Kimchi is made of the combination of radishes, turnips, scallions, garlic, ginger, chili pepper and seafood. Consuming kimchi is a Korean and it is known that every Korean person consumes about one quarter of kimchi on a daily basis.

5. Mead

Mead is a very popular type of wine made with honey and it is believed to be the first and the most ancient honey wine that humankind had ever known. Mead was first discovered by a hunter more than 12,000 years ago. Since then, humans started using honey with wine.

6. Kombucha

Kombucha, which is the main theme of our book, is a fermented drink that dates back to Chin in Qing Dynasty. Kombucha later became very popular and started spreading into many parts of the world.

Chapter 4: Types and Variations of Kombucha Tea

To prepare fresh and tasty tea leaves for kombucha, we need tea to ferment it and we call the obtained tea real tea rather than herbal tea. This type of tea may be sensitive to the strong fragrant oils, too. For example, we can find a type of tea that resembles Earl Grey and it is characterized by containing Bergamot oil which can kill the culture or harm it. We can also distinguish between other types of tea that can grant us various results that can affect the taste of tea and change it from a light taste to an unexpected cider taste. Below is a list of the main types of teas that we can use to brew kombucha.

1. Oolong Tea

Oolong tea is half-way between green tea and black tea. It's gently rolled after picking and allowed to partially ferment until the edges of the leaves start to turn brown. Oolong combines the taste and color of black and green tea.

2. Black Tea

Black tea is a very popular type of tea that is known for its leaves that are completely fermented. The leaves are spread out in the air and then left to be naturally wilted before starting to fire the leaves and to brew it into a delicious rich taste of amber.

3. Green Tea

Who doesn't know green tea? It is the number one tea used in different culinary traditions and it is even sacred in many religions. To prepare green tea, we have to wither it first; then we steam or heat it in order to prevent the oxidation of the tea and after that, the tea leaves are rolled, then dried. It is also characterized by a very delicious taste, with a light green color. The Japanese Sencha tea is used to make a special high–quality kombucha.

4. The White Tea

You might not have heard of the white tea because white tea is one of the highest–quality teas. White tea is very rare to find and very delicate to prepare; it is generally plucked for about forty-eight hours between the time its buds become mature and the time it opens. The main difference between black, green and white tea is that white tea is neither steamed nor rolled, but it is usually dried in the open air and in the sun. This drying method helps preserve most of the antioxidant proprieties that are beneficial for health. Indeed, white tea contains more antioxidants like polyphenols than are in green tea.

Chapter 5: How to Grow Scoby

If you are a beginner to making kombucha, but you don't know how to make a scoby, you won't get the kombucha you imagine. So if you are excited to prepare your own homemade kombucha, start by learning how to make your kombucha.

Kombucha is the most delicious, tangy and sweet fermented type of drink that you will easily get addicted to. And if you are hesitating because you don't know how to make kombucha at home, just start reading and follow the instructions and you will be easily able to come up with a very tasty kombucha. What are you waiting for? Plunge into the world of kombucha, but first you should be able to distinguish between two main classes of fermentation. The first class of fermentation is characterized by being wild and it relies on the natural way of making bacteria in our environment. The second form of the process of fermentation is the one we need to add the culture, or the starter, to anything we want to ferment. The scoby is made of yeast and bacteria, and to this combination we add the sweet tea to catalyze and ignite the process of fermentation. There are, indeed, two diverse ways to grow the scoby you need to make kombucha.

1. Pour 1 cup of mainstream kombucha in a mason jar.

2. Cover the jar with a woven cloth and make sure to seal it tightly; then set it aside at troom temperature out of everybody's reach.

3. You will notice that the kombucha will begin to grow the scoby

Note: If you are new to scoby, you can start with a very thin film and then it will develop into a disk that resembles jelly.

Chapter 6: Kombucha Equipments

1. Glass

If you wonder what the best option for you to brew your own kombucha is, you won't find better than a glass container. Using a glass container will prevent the reaction to the acidity of your brew and it won't be scratched easily, either. Besides, the prices of glass containers are affordable. You can also use storage jars or canning jars. Make sure that the inner spigot is made of plastic and beware of using metal containers because it can harm your kombucha!

2. Ceramic

If you prefer using a ceramic container to brew kombucha, you should ensure that the glaze is food-grade so that you can avoid any contact with the lead.

3. Porcelain:

Porcelain is generally known for being used in brewing the kombucha tea, as long as you avoid the food-grade porcelain pieces. Porcelain is known for being made of clay that has a quality that resembles paste. This clay is used to produce a white-like product called porcelain.

4. Cover the Kombucha with a container

To ferment the kombucha tea, you need to keep it away from flies and critters. And to make sure that you protect your kombucha jar, you should cover it with the container you use with. There are several criteria you should consider in choosing the lid to use.

a. A filter or a weave towel, sealed with a rubber band is a perfect choice.

b. Using butter muslin makes a great choice too; you can cut it into a layer that covers the top of your container.

c. Storing or canning jar rings are very suitable to enable you to seal the fabric over the tops of jars.

5. Mesh Tea Ball

Mesh Tea Balls are very useful for brewing Kombucha.

6. Use a Funnel

Using a funnel with finished kombucha brew is very helpful to facilitate your task in making homemade kombucha.

7. A Stick-On Thermometer

Temperature has always been known for playing an important role in making a home-brewed kombucha. The kombucha culture works best when it is placed at room temperature. Stick-thermometers are easy to use and help you watch the temperature of your kombucha.

Steps of Brewing Kombucha

Whether you are new to making kombucha at home or you are an expert, there are still things you need to learn before brewing your own kombucha.

• You need to buy a scoby or obtain it from an acquaintance.

• You need time and patience to brew the kombucha.

• You should estimate the quantity of kombucha you have to brew.

1. The first step in brewing kombucha

You should start by boiling a quantity that is estimated by half of the amount of boiled water. Then add the sugar to the water and then stir it until it is completely dissolved. Add the tea bags to your hot water. Set the tea aside to steep and after that add the second half of the water to facilitate the cooling process. Set the tea aside to cool.

2. Second Step:

Add the cooled tea to a container of your choice; but don't add the scoby immediately; it may risk killing the culture if the tea is too hot. Slide the scoby into your tea and cover your container with a cloth; then secure the lid with the help of a rubber band. Set the kombucha aside and leave it for about seven to ten days.

3. Third Step:

Set the tea aside to ferment for around 10 days at a temperature of 70F. After about seven days, taste your kombucha and see if it has the fermentation taste that you desire; don't insert any metal or iron spoons and just use your finger. If you prefer a taste that resembles that of vinegar, let it ferment for a longer time. You can consume your kombucha with fruits, spices, beers, wines, and muddled fruits.

4. Fourth Step:

Once the kombucha tastes the way you like, you can bottle it for a second round of fermentation. You can use the Grolsch style flip top bottles and make sure to avoid the use of metal containers. You can transfer the kombucha with a funnel.

Chapter 7: Benefits of Kombucha

Because it is a completely natural beverage, kombucha is considered one of the healthiest drinks ever. Many scientific as well as nutrition studies have discovered various benefits that are associated with brewing kombucha. However, the effects of kombucha on our bodies differ from a person to another according to different proprieties. And because kombucha has proved its positive effect and thanks to its various benefits, the consumption of kombucha spread all over the globe. Below are some important benefits:

1. Digestive benefit

The antioxidant power of the historical kombucha has great digestive benefits to the health, mainly because of the high levels of probiotics, acid and enzymes, too. Many studies have proven that kombucha helps heal the effects of stomach ulcers and in some cases, it even prevents ulcers. Kombucha has also proven to be a very effective medication that has the same effect as Prilosec, a medication that is generally prescribed for medical cases like GERD and heartburn.

2. Helps in detoxification

Kombucha has always been known for its high detoxification power; it makes a perfect example of the ability of kombucha in counteracting the toxicity that may affect our liver. A study has discovered that kombucha helps in protecting from any oxidative situation that may not be healed with ordinary physiology.

3. Immune Health

The consumption of kombucha is responsible for modulating the immune system and it is known for its high ability to control free radicals. Kombucha drinks have proven their power to reduce the oxidative effect as well as the immune stress. Scientists have also been able to notice the presence of vitamin C in the kombucha beverage. Kombucha is also known for its ability to protect the body against the damage of cells, tumors and some inflammatory issues.

4. Energy

Kombucha is known for its richness in iron that is released from the black tea leaves during the process of fermentation. Kombucha beverages are also characterized by containing small amounts of vitamin b and caffeine, which help in energizing the body. The iron that is released from kombucha increases the quantity of haemoglobin in the blood and stimulates the production of energy in the level of the cells.

5. Preventing Cancer

Kombucha beverages are very beneficial for their power to prevent cancer and it also helps to recover from it. Indeed, kombucha contains an acid called glucaric acid and consuming this acid decreases the risk of cancer. The American records proved that President Reagan consumed kombucha to fight the cancer that affected his stomach.

6. Kombucha helps in weight loss

Studies and researchers have found that kombucha helps in improving the metabolism within our body and doesn't allow the accumulation of fat. Kombucha is rich in polyphenols and in acetic acid, which help decrease weight.

7. Kombucha prevents the damage of joints

Kombucha has always been known for its ability to heal and prevent joint damage in various ways. Kombucha is high in the presence of glucosamine and it helps increase the production of synovial hyaluronic acid. The presence of this acid helps support the preservation of the collagen and protects us from arthritic problems. It also soothes joint pain. Kombucha also helps to prevent wrinkles and keeps our skin fresh.

Chapter 8: Delicious Kombucha Recipes

If you have never tasted Kombucha in your life, it is time you experience this delicious ingredient.

Recipe 1: Kombucha with Ginger flavor

(Time: 40 minutes\ Servings: 1)

INGREDIENTS:

- 3 and ½ quarts of water
- 1 cup of white sugar
- 4 bags of black tea
- 4 bags of green tea or you can use 1 tablespoon of loose green tea.
- 2 cups of pre-made unflavored kombucha
- 1 scoby per each fermentation jar

- 3 inch piece of fresh ginger

DIRECTIONS:

1. You will need about 6 glass bottles that are 16-oz with swing top bottles and also with plastic lids.

2. Start by boiling the water, then remove it off the heat and add the sugar and stir until it is dissolved.

3. Drop in your tea and let it steep until your water becomes completely cool. This process needs several hours.

4. Once your tea has cooled, strain the tea or remove the tea bags; then add your premade kombucha.

5. Now, pour the obtained mixture into a glass jar, then slide your scoby right on top with your clean hands.

6. Cover the jar with layers of clean paper towers, then secure it with a rubber band.

7. Keep your fermenting kombucha away from sunlight and make sure the place you keep it in is at room temperature.

8. Let the Kombucha ferment for about 8 to 10 days and keep checking on the scoby from time to time.

9. After about 7 to 8 days, you can start testing your kombucha everyday and when it reaches the desired sweetness then the kombucha is ready to be consumed.

10. Clean your hands; then gently lift your scoby and place it on a plate so that you can make another batch of kombucha. Scrub your ginger clean, but don't peel it. Finely grate the ginger or just chop with a food processor. Don't spill the ginger juice and keep it to be used later.

11. Divide the grated ginger between your bottles and pour your fermented kombucha in the bottles; then store it for about 2 to 3 days out of sunlight.

12. Refrigerate the kombucha for about 4 hours, then strain and serve it with ginger bits.

Recipe 2: Kombucha Tea

(Time: 35 minutes\ Servings: 8)

INGREDIENTS:

- 2 cups of any kombucha of your choice
- 3 quarts of distilled water
- 1 cup of organic fine table sugar
- 3 to 4 organic black tea bags
- 2 to 3 green tea bags (organic)

DIRECTIONS:

1. Boil the 3 quarts of distilled water and when you are done, set it aside to cool.

2. Put the organic tea bags and the green tea bags into the water; then let it steep for about 15 minutes.

3. Remove your tea bags and then add about 1 cup of sugar to it.

4. Set the sweetened tea aside to cool; then place the scoby, the 2 cups of your kombucha and the sweetened tea into a glass container.

5. Cover your container by using a flour sack cloth; then secure the bottle with a rubber band.

6. Place your container in a cupboard or just another place out of reach in your house and set it aside to brew for about 10 days.

7. When your kombucha has attained the desired thickness, you can pour it into glass bottles with a funnel to consume it later.

8. Serve and enjoy your kombucha!

Recipe 3: Kombucha tea

(Time: 15 minutes\ Servings: 7)

INGREDIENTS:

- 1 gallon of homemade kombucha
- 3 cups of extra pulp orange juice
- To prepare the orange creamsicle use 16 oz of homemade orange flavored kombucha
- 3 tablespoons of canned coconut milk

DIRECTIONS:

1. Transfer about half of your homemade kombucha and add to it half of your orange juice. Then, add the ingredients to the ½ gallon of pitcher and stir very well.

2. Pour your orange kombucha into sanitized glass bottles of 16-oz and set it aside to steep in a dark place or in your cupboard for about 3 days.

3. Place your bottles in your refrigerator and refrigerate the kombucha until it is completely chilled.

4. Open one of the bottles of your orange kombucha drink and be careful when you open it.

5. With a strainer, strain your kombucha into glasses and add about 3 tbsp of the coconut milk; then mix very well and enjoy your orange kombucha!

Recipe 4: Oregano Chamomile Kombucha

(Time: 20 minutes\ Servings: 7)

INGREDIENTS:

- 1 gallon of filtered water
- 2 teaspoons of yerba mate
- 6 teaspoons of loose tea
- 1 cup of organic white cane sugar
- 2 cups of starter unflavoured kombucha with green tea

- ½ teaspoon of dried sage
- ¼ cup of dried chamomile flowers
- 1 teaspoon of dried oregano
- 1 teaspoon of dried basil
- 1 cup of agave syrup

DIRECTIONS:

1. Start by boiling the water; then steep the green tea with the yerba mate for about 20 minutes.

2. Add the white cane sugar and let it cool at room temperature.

3. Remove the obtained tea and after that, transfer your liquid to the container you have prepared for brewing.

4. Add the SCOBY and the starter.

5. In the primary fermentation process, check the kombucha flavour starting from the fourth day and if the flavour is still sweet, try removing the scoby and set aside about two cups of the tea to use in the following batch.

6. During the second fermentation process, wrap your dried herbs with a muslin or clean cotton white cloth.

7. Seal the top of the bottle with a rubber bundle and cover your brewing container again.

8. Let the kombucha sit for an entire night at room temperature and then add the agave syrup; then fill your bottles and set them aside for at least one and half days.

9. Store your bottles in the refrigerator for about 4 hours.

10. Serve and enjoy your kombucha!

Recipe 5: Pumpkin Kombucha

(Time: 15 minutes\ Servings: 8)

INGREDIENTS:

- 1 gallon of filtered water
- ¾ cup of organic white cane sugar
- ½ cup of pure maple syrup
- 8 teaspoons of loose oolong tea
- 2 cups of unflavoured kombucha black tea starter
- 1 tablespoon of ground nutmeg
- 1 tablespoon of ground allspice

- 1 tablespoon of ground cinnamon
- 1 tablespoon of dried ground ginger

DIRECTIONS:

1. Boil your water and remove it from the heat; then add the sugar with ¼ cup of maple syrup.

2. Stir in the tea and let the ingredients steep for about 15 minutes.

3. Remove your tea and set it aside until it is room temperature.

4. Transfer your liquid to your brewing container and add the starter, then the scoby.

5. For the primary fermentation, you can check the flavour on the fourth or the fifth fermentation day.

6. If the kombucha is still sweet on the fifth day, try removing the scoby and then remove about 2 cups of the tea for your next batch.

7. For the secondary fermentation process, mix your ground spices with half a cup of the maple syrup in a wide container; then add the kombucha tea.

8. Close your container and put it in a dark place in your house for about two days.

9. Strain your tea into glass bottles and then store it in the refrigerator for about a month.

10. Consume your delicious kombucha!

Recipe 6: Peach Kombucha

(Time: 15 minutes\ Servings: 8)

INGREDIENTS:

- 1 gallon of filtered water
- 1 cup of organic white cane sugar
- 1 tablespoon of unsulphured molasses
- 6 bags of black tea or 6 teaspoons of loose tea
- 2 bags of oolong tea
- 2 cups of starter
- 2 cups of sliced fresh or frozen peaches

- 1 tablespoon of whole black peppercorns
- ½ cup of fresh basil leaves

DIRECTIONS:

1. Boil your water and then remove it from the heat, and toss in the molasses and the sugar

2. Pour in the tea and steep it until your liquid gets cool at room temperature.

3. Remove your tea and transfer your obtained liquid to your brewing container.

4. Add your starter and your scoby.

5. For the primary fermentation, check the flavour of the kombucha on the third day and if the kombucha is still sweet, remove the scoby and remove around 2 cups of tea for your next batch.

6. For the secondary fermentation, add the peppercorns, the fresh basil leaves, and the peaches to your brewing container; then tightly seal the lid.

7. Place your kombucha in a dark place in your house and leave it for about 3 days; try releasing the lid periodically so that you can get rid of any carbonation

8. Seal your bottles and store in your refrigerator for about a week

9. Serve and enjoy your peach kombucha!

Recipe 7: Carrot Kombucha

(Time: 20 minutes\ Servings: 6-7)

INGREDIENTS:

- 1 gallon of filtered water
- ½ cup of organic white cane sugar
- ½ cup and ¼ cup of agave syrup
- 8 teaspoons of hochija tea or loose tea
- 2 cups of unflavored kombucha made from green tea
- 1 cup of freshly grated carrots
- 1 cup of freshly grated beets

- 1 cup of bottled hot sauce

DIRECTIONS:

1. Start by boiling the water, then remove it from the heat and add the cane sugar.

2. Add ½ cup of the agave syrup.

3. Pour in the tea and let the Kombucha steep until it is room temperature.

4. Remove your tea from the kombucha and transfer the obtained liquid to your brewing container with the scoby and the starter.

5. For the primary fermentation, you can check your kombucha flavor on the second day of fermentation because of the effect of the agave.

6. If your kombucha is too sweet, remove two cups of your tea for your next batch.

7. For the secondary fermentation, add the grated carrots and the beets into your brewing container and close the lid.

8. Set the kombucha aside for about two days away from sunlight; then start checking the kombucha every day for any excess carbonation.

9. Add two dashes of hot sauce into your bottles and close the lids; then store the bottles in the refrigerator for about 10 days

Recipe8: Mango Kombucha

(Time: 30 minutes\ Servings: 7-8)

INGREDIENTS:

- 1 gallon of filtered water
- ½ cup of organic white cane sugar
- ½cup of coconut sugar
- 4 bags of green tea or 4 teaspoons loose tea
- 4 bags of rooibos tea
- 2 cups of starter

- 1 cup of fresh mango cut into chunks
- ½ cup of tangerine juice
- tablespoon of lime juice
- teaspoon of lemon juice

DIRECTIONS:

1. Start by boiling the water and then remove it from the heat.

2. Add the white sugar and about ½ cup of coconut sugar.

3. Pour in the tea and let it steep for a period of time or until the tea becomes room temperature.

4. Remove your tea, then transfer your obtained liquid to a brewing container. Next, add the scoby and the starter.

5. For the primary fermentation; check the flavour of your kombucha after one day.

6. If the kombucha is very sweet, remove two cups of tea and set it aside to use it for the next batch of kombucha.

7. For the secondary fermentation, toss in the mango chunks to your brewing container and add ½ cup of coconut sugar with the remaining fruit juice.

8. Cover your brewing container once more with a clean cloth and set it aside in a dark spot for about 3 days.

9. Strain the obtained tea into bottles and let it chill in your refrigerator for about 2 hours.

10. Serve and enjoy your kombucha; you can also store the kombucha for 9 days in the refrigerator.

Recipe 9: Strawberry Kombucha

(Time: 20 minutes\ Servings: 5-6)

INGREDIENTS:

- 1 gallon of filtered water
- 1 cup of raw organic sugar crystals
- 6 teaspoon of loose green tea
- 2 bags of black tea
- 2 cups of starter
- 1 cup of crushed strawberries

- 1 vanilla bean
- ½ cup of clover honey
- 2 teaspoons of almond extract

DIRECTIONS:

1. Boil the quantity of water and remove it from the heat, then add the sugar and the tea and set it aside to steep.

2. Transfer your obtained liquid to your brewing container and add the scoby and the starter.

3. For the primary fermentation, you can start checking your kombucha flavor starting from the 5th day and when you notice your kombucha is still sweet, remove the developed scoby and set aside about 2 cups of your tea for your next batch.

4. For the secondary fermentation, add the vanilla bean to your brewing container and add the honey, the crushed strawberries, and the extract of almond. Seal your container with a tight lid and put it into a dark place for about three days.

5. Strain your tea into glass bottles, then seal your bottles and after that store it in a refrigerator for up to about 10 days.

6. Serve and enjoy your Strawberry Kombucha!

Recipe 10: Cranberry Kombucha

(Time: 10 minutes\ Servings: 4)

INGREDIENTS:

- 32 oz of cherry or berry kombucha
- 2 large sliced large oranges
- 1 cup of fresh cranberries
- Use cinnamon sugar for the rims

DIRECTIONS:

1. Fill a glass container with sliced cranberries and oranges, then add your kombucha and stir very well to combine the ingredients.

2. Wet the rims of the glasses and dip them in all the cinnamon sugar.

3. Fill your glasses with ice and top it all with kombucha and fruits.

4. Serve and enjoy!

Recipe 11: Kombucha with Fruits and Green Tea

(Time: 15 minutes\ Servings: 6)

INGREDIENTS:

• 1 gallon of filtered water

• 8 teaspoons of loose green tea

• 1 cup of organic white cane sugar

• 2 cups of unflavored kombucha made of green or black tea

• 20 oz can of lychee fruit in the syrup

• 1 cup of the syrup of the lychee fruit

- 8 star anise

DIRECTIONS:

1. Boil your water and then remove it from the heat and add to it tea.

2. Let the ingredients steep for about 30 minutes, then remove the tea and stir the white cane sugar. Let the liquid cool to room temperature, transfer the liquid to the brewing container, then add the starter and the scoby.

3. For the primary fermentation, start tasting and checking the flavor right on the third day and if the kombucha is too sweet, remove your scoby and take out two cups of tea to use for the next batch.

4. For the secondary fermentation, place 1 lychee fruit into every bottle, then add around 1 cup of your syrup to your kombucha tea. Stir very well.

5. Place 1 star anise in every bottle you use; then fill your glass bottles with your kombucha tea.

6. Seal your bottles, and set aside at the room temperature for about 2 to 3 days.

7. Store the kombucha in the fridge, then serve and enjoy it!

Recipe 12: Blueberry Kombucha with Mint

(Time: 10 minutes\ Servings: 5)

INGREDIENTS:

- 10 crushed mint leaves
- ½ cup of frozen blueberries
- 12 oz of flavored blueberry kombucha tea

- Ice cubes
- Distilled water
- ½ cup of maple syrup

DIRECTIONS:

1. Divide the leaves of mint equally and then place them into the bottom of your glasses.

2. With a wooden spoon, crush your mint leaves or chop them into tiny pieces; then crush them with the knife before adding.

3. Apply the same process with the blueberries and gently crush them.

4. Fill your glasses with ice cubes and pour the kombucha in.

5. Fill the glasses with the sparkling water and serve.

6. Enjoy the kombucha!

Recipe 13: Kombucha Cocktail

(Time: 12 minutes\ Servings: 4-5)

INGREDIENTS:

- 1 gallon of filtered water
- 4 bags of black tea
- 4 teaspoons of jasmine green tea
- 1 cup of organic white cane sugar
- 2 cups of starter
- 2 tablespoons of organic dried lavender buds
- ½ cup of light honey
- 1 teaspoon of rose water

DIRECTIONS:

1. Boil the gallon of water and remove it from the heat, then add the white cane sugar.

2. Pour in the tea and keep the bags separate from each other.

3. After about 15 minutes, remove the black tea and let the green tea steep at room temperature until it is completely chilled.

4. Remove the tea and transfer the obtained liquid to your brewing container with the scoby and the starter.

5. For the primary fermentation, start tasting the flavor of your kombucha starting from the fourth day and when the kombucha is not too sweet, remove your scoby and remove about 2 cups of tea for your next batch.

6. For the secondary fermentation, put the buds of lavender into a muslin bag or a tea ball, then add it to the container set for brewing.

7. Cover your container with a clean cloth and set it aside overnight; then add the honey and the rose water with the lavender.

8. Pour your kombucha into glass bottles and tightly seal the bottles; then set them aside in a dark place for a period of two to three days.

9. Store your kombucha in the refrigerator for seven days.

Recipe 14: Cucumber Kombucha

(Time: 10 minutes\ Servings: 1)
INGREDIENTS:

- 3 cucumber slices
- 2 small strawberries
- ¾ cup of original kombucha
- 5 ice cubes

DIRECTIONS:

1. In a large glass, mix all together the strawberry with the cucumber and stir very well.

2. Fill your glass with the ice cubes and add your kombucha tea, then stir with a spoon

3. Serve your kombucha and add cucumber slices

4. Enjoy the cucumber kombucha!

Recipe 15: Blackberry Kombucha

(Time: 10 minutes\ Servings: 4-5)

INGREDIENTS:

- 1 gallon of filtered water
- 1 cup of organic white cane sugar
- 4 teaspoons of loose tea
- 2 cups of unflavoured kombucha made of black tea
- 2 bags of Earl Grey tea
- ½ cup of honey
- 2 cups of fresh or frozen blackberries
- 1/8 teaspoon of grey sea salt

DIRECTIONS:

1. Start by boiling the water, then remove it from the heat.

2. Add the white cane sugar and pour in the white tea and let steep for about 15 minutes.

3. Add your black tea and set the liquid aside at room temperature until it cools.

4. Remove your tea and transfer the obtained liquid to your clean brewing container.

5. Add the scoby and the starter.

6. For the primary fermentation, start checking the taste of the kombucha flavour starting from the fifth day and if your kombucha is very sweet, remove about 2 cups of the tea and keep it for your next batch.

7. For the second fermentation, add the tea bags to your brewing container and add the honey, the blackberries, and the sea salt.

8. Seal your container with a lid, then set it aside at room temperature for about two days.

9. Strain your kombucha tea into clean glass bottles and let it chill in your refrigerator, then store it for 9 days.

10. Serve and enjoy your kombucha!

Recipe 16: Apple Kombucha

(Time: 15 minutes\ Servings: 3)

INGREDIENTS:

- 4 teaspoons of black tea
- 4 teaspoons of green tea
- ½ cup of refined white sugar
- 6 cups of distilled water
- ½ glass container; gallon sized
- Large apple
- 2 sticks of cinnamon
- ½ teaspoon of finely ground cloves

- Piece of clean cloth
- A rubber band

DIRECTIONS:

1. Boil the water on your stove.

2. Pour the water in a glass container and add the tea to it, then stir and add the sugar. Mix very well.

3. Set the tea aside until it has cooled; then remove the tea leaves with a strainer.

4. Add the scoby and cover the container with a clean piece of cloth; then seal it with a rubber band around its top.

5. Set the kombucha aside in a dark place in your house for about 8 to 10 days and after the 7th day, start tasting the kombucha to see if it is adjusted to the flavor you want.

6. Once the taste is perfect, remove the scoby to use it for a new batch of kombucha or store it in a container.

7. Pour the kombucha in glass container with a little bit of scoby, then place it in the refrigerator. Meanwhile, cut the apple into small chunks and add it to your kombucha; then add the spices.

8. Set the kombucha in the refrigerator for about three days.

Recipe 17: Beer Kombucha

(Time: 15 minutes\ Servings: 2-3)

INGREDIENTS:

- ¼ cup of sarsaparilla root
- ¼ teaspoon of wintergreen leaf a compulsory ingredient)
- ½ cup of unrefined cane organic sugar
- 1 teaspoon of vanilla extract
- 6 cups of filtered water
- 2 tbsp of lime juice

DIRECTIONS:

1. Start by putting the sarsaparilla root and the wintergreen leaf into a medium pot and add to it the distilled water; then raise the heat to high.

2. Boil your ingredients and then lower the heat and let it simmer for about 20 minutes.

3. Strain your liquid with a mesh strainer and while it is still warm, toss in the sugar, the molasses, the vanilla, and the lime juice; then stir very well until your ingredients are dissolved.

4. Add about ½ cup of your root beer liquid to each 14 oz of your kombucha.

5. Add raisins to your kombucha and slices of ginger to the bottles and place it in the refrigerator for about 5 hours.

6. Serve and enjoy your kombucha!

Recipe 18: Kombucha Candies

(Time: 30 minutes\ Servings: 2)

INGREDIENTS:

- A kombucha scoby
- A quantity of sugar that equals the kombucha
- 1 dash of lemon juice
- Lemon zest
- White sugar

DIRECTIONS:

1. Rinse your scoby to remove any stringy things.

2. Dice the scoby with clean scissors or with a very sharp knife.

3. Gently combine your scoby squares with the sugar, and around 1 tablespoon of lemon juice.

4. Boil your ingredients over medium heat in a large saucepan for about 10 minutes.

5. Remove your pot from the stove and remove your candies from the heat; then place it above a baking sheet lined with a parchment paper.

6. Let your syrup chill for about 15 minutes, then pour the syrup over your candies and set aside until it becomes thick.

7. Bake your candies at about 350° F for 10 minutes.

8. Remove the candies and set aside to cool.

9. Serve and enjoy your scoby candies!

Recipe 19: Kombucha Ketchup

(Time: 10 minutes\ Servings: 3)

INGREDIENTS:

- 12 oz of tomato paste
- ½ cup of kombucha
- ¼ cup of rapadura
- 2 teaspoons of molasses
- ½ teaspoons of sea salt

- 1 pinch of nutmeg
- 1 pinch of cinnamon
- 1 pinch of clove
- 1 pinch of allspice

DIRECTIONS:

1. In a clean and wide bowl, whisk altogether all of your ingredients except for the water

2. Add your kombucha to the ketchup and put it in a jar

3. You may freeze your kombucha in tiny batches

4. Use your ketchup kombucha and enjoy its taste!

Recipe 20: Kombucha Cookies

(Time: 20 minutes\ Servings: 5)

INGREDIENTS:

- 1 cup of organic softened butter
- ¼ cup of karma kombucha
- 1 cup of organic cane sugar
- 1 teaspoon of baking soda
- 1 and ½ cups of organic white whole wheat flour

- ½ cup of hemp seed
- ¼ cup of chopped walnuts

DIRECTIONS:

1. Preheat your oven to about 325° F.

2. Cream your butter and add the sugar to a bowl with the help of a mixer.

3. Sift in the flour and the baking soda altogether with the butter and the mixture of the sugar.

4. Add the kombucha and stir in the seeds or the nuts.

5. Add 1 teaspoon of the mixture over a greased cookie sheet.

6. Bake your kombucha cake for about 20 minutes

7. Serve and enjoy your cake!

Recipe 21: Kombucha bread

(Time: 20 minutes\ Servings: 5)

INGREDIENTS:

- 1 and ½ cup of KT dregs from the bottom of a jar
- 1 and ½ cups of flour
- ½ cup of vinegar
- 2 tbsp of filtered water
- 1 tablespoon of yeast

DIRECTIONS:

1. Sanitize a large bowl with the distilled vinegar and the filtered water.

2. Add the flour and the KT to your bowl.

3. Mix your ingredients until they are very well combined.

4. Cover the flour with a cloth and set it aside for about 24 hours.

5. Check your starter for any appearance of bubbles; then add about ½ cup of flour.

6. Bake your bread for about 25 minutes.

7. Serve and enjoy your kombucha bread!

Recipe 22: Kombucha Brownies

(Time: 10 minutes\ Servings: 8)

INGREDIENTS:

- 1 and ½ cups of Besan flour
- 1 teaspoon of baking powder
- 6 tablespoons of unsweetened cocoa powder
- 1 pinch of salt
- 1 and ¼ cup of brown sugar
- 4 large eggs

- 2 teaspoons of vanilla extract
- ¾ cup of coconut milk
- 3 teaspoons of kombucha
- ½ cup of mild olive oil

DIRECTIONS:

1. Preheat your oven to about 320° F and grease a spring baking tin.

2. In a deep and wide bowl, sift in the Besan flour, the baking powder, the cocoa powder, the salt and the sugar.

3. In another bowl, mix together your eggs with the vanilla extract, the coconut milk, the kombucha and the oil until it is emulsified.

4. Make a hole in the centre of your dry ingredients then add your wet ingredients and mix until you obtain a very well-incorporated mixture.

5. Pour the batter into your greased baking tray and bake it for about 1 hour and 5 minutes.

6. Remove from the oven, then let it cool for 10 minutes.

7. Serve and enjoy your brownies with sugar dust!

Recipe 23: Kombucha Carrot Cake

(Time: 40 minutes\ Servings: 4)

INGREDIENTS:

- 5 and ¼ cups of grated carrots
- ½ cup of ground flax seed
- ¾ cup of warm water
- 2 and ½ cups of flour
- ½ teaspoons of cardamom
- 1 teaspoon of cinnamon

- ½ teaspoon of salt
- 1 and ¼ teaspoon of baking soda
- 1 and ¼ teaspoon of baking powder
- 1 and ¼ cup of cane sugar
- ¾ cup of brown sugar
- 1 teaspoon of vanilla
- ½ cup of unsweetened applesauce
- 1 cup of melted coconut oil
- For your frosting, use ¾ cup of coconut oil, ¼ cup of cocoa butter, 10 tablespoons of plain kombucha, and 3 cups of powdered sugar.

DIRECTIONS:

1. Preheat your oven to about 350°F and grease three baking pans.

2. In the bowl of your mixer, mix altogether the flax and the warm water; then set aside your ingredients until they thicken.

3. In another large bowl, combine the flour, the spice salt, the spices, the baking soda and the baking powder.

4. Add the sugars, the applesauce, and the vanilla to the mixture and stir very well.

5. While the mixer is running, pour in the coconut oil and mix.

6. Add your dry ingredients and combine very well; then add the grated carrots.

7. Divide the obtained dough between your already greased pans.

8. Bake the carrot cakes for about 30 minutes.

9. Remove the cake from the oven and set it aside to cool for about 10 minutes. Meanwhile, prepare the frosting and start by heating your coconut oil and the cocoa butter to boiling for about 5 minutes.

10. Set the mixture aside and soften your butter to room temperature.

11. Cream your butter with a mixer until it becomes fluffy and add 2 and ½ tablespoons of kombucha with 1 cup of the powdered sugar and keep stirring

12. Continue adding the sugar and the kombucha

13. Decorate the cake with the frosting, then serve and enjoy!

Recipe 24: Grapes Kombucha

(Time: 10 minutes\ Servings: 2)

INGREDIENTS:

- 1 cup of red grapes
- 16 oz bottle of grape kombucha

DIRECTIONS:

1. Put a quantity of red grapes in a pan.
2. Pour the grape kombucha over the top of grapes.

3. Put the ingredients in the freezer for around 20 minutes.

4. Break the frozen ingredients with the help of a fork and then leave it aside.

5. Freeze the ingredients for about 30 minutes.

6. Put the ingredients into a glass and serve.

7. Serve in glasses and enjoy a fresh taste!

Recipe 25: Kombucha Salad

(Time: 5 minutes\ Servings: 2-3)

INGREDIENTS:

- 1 cup of kombucha
- 1 and ½ cups of olive oil
- Finely minced garlic cloves
- 1 and ½ tablespoons of minced onion
- 1 tablespoon of honey
- 1 tablespoon of dried oregano
- ½ teaspoon of dried basil
- 1 and ½ tablespoons of fresh minced parsley

- 1 tablespoon of sea salt
- ¼ teaspoon of red pepper flakes

DIRECTIONS:

1. Mix all of your ingredients in a glass jar, then cover it and shake all of your ingredients until they are combined.

2. You need to shake from time to time before pouring the dressing over the salad.

3. Serve and enjoy your salad with kombucha!

Chapter 9: Kombucha Tips

Making kombucha at home has a variety of benefits, like being able to taste your own kombucha and adjust it to your favourite flavour. In order to find new blends and to impress yourself and your family with your homemade kombucha, you need to know some tips that will make brewing kombucha easier.

1. Choose your tea with extra care.

Choosing the type of the tea you use when your start brewing your kombucha is very important to its flavour. Tea differs from black to green to white and each has its own influence on the taste of kombucha, so you should try using a different type of tea and adjust its taste to the flavour you prefer.

2. Use distilled water to brew your kombucha

It is advisable to use distilled water when you decide to make your homemade kombucha because using tap water will harm the kombucha beverage. Besides, ordinary home filtration systems can't remove the presence of fungicides or any chemical additives.

3. Choose refined table sugar

You might think that using refined sugar is not good for your kombucha, but you should know that it is your best choice in making kombucha. Indeed, refined table sugar is characterized by being rich in nutrients and vitamins. Studies have found that using honey or other sweeteners doesn't work as well.

4. Choose your brewing container

If you are wondering which brewing container you need to use, the answer is simple. You need a mouthed glass container or jar to brew your kombucha. You can also use a mason jar or a cookie jar, but be careful of using a plastic container. And remember, the wider the top of your jar is, the faster the kombucha is going to brew.

5. Use one or more black tea bags because of its ability to provide the kombucha with a high amount of tannin. Using green tea is also possible, but you should be careful of using any type of decaffeinated and most importantly, don't use herbal tea.

6. Let the tea cool before the process of brewing

Let your tea cool for about two hours before brewing kombucha because using hot tea may cause harm the kombucha and makes it mold.

7. Try making your kombucha in a bowl

Have you ever tried brewing kombucha in a bowl? if you haven't tried it, it is the right time to give it a try. Making kombucha in a bowl is a very good alternative for using containers. Kombucha also needs a container with a wider top in comparison to its depth. Just make sure to use a plain, clean and clear glass bowl.

8. Straining kombucha

When you are finished with fermenting kombucha, you should strain it, but when doing that, don't use a coffee filter because there will be a risk that it will leave chemicals. Sometimes, you don't even have to strain the kombucha and use a cotton cloth or shirt to cover the kombucha container.

9. Flavour your kombucha

When the fermentation period is finished and once you have removed the scoby, you can add flavours of your choice to the kombucha and consume it or even ferment it for a longer time.

10. Make sure to clean the brewers

Clean your brewers after brewing batches of kombucha so that you can keep the dead yeast to the lowest amount.

11. What to do when kombucha is incomplete in the middle?

When the kombucha is not complete in its middle, tear it a little bit of it in the middle, then continue brewing it.

12. Warm temperature

By making sure the temperature is warm, the kombucha will grow faster and brewing it will become easier. Be careful of cold temperatures because it will slow down the brewing process and it may completely stop when the temperature falls below the degree of 60° F.

13. Storing scoby

If you need to store scoby for a determined period of time, try placing it into a jar and pour on it some kombucha tea; then cover the jar with the help of a tight lid. Keep in mind that scoby is known for surviving for many weeks.

14. Store your fermentation away from the sunlight

You need to start the fermentation away from the sunlight; you can use the counter of your refrigerator, but don't hide it somewhere you would forget about.

15. Filling the container of kombucha

You should fill the kombucha container at about 10% so that you can ensure a fast fermentation process. If you want to make the growing process of the scoby faster, you can raise the culture amount to about 30% of the capacity of the container.

Chapter 10: Common Kombucha Mistakes

If you are a beginner in making homemade kombucha, and if you are dealing with many errors and mistakes, the following tips will help. Have a look at the different mistakes you can make so that you can avoid them in the future and to keep your kombucha healthy.

1. Don't use cheesecloth to cover your kombucha container, but you can rather choose to use a white cotton and thin cheesecloth. It is also okay to use a flour sack towel or if you don't have it, you can use a white and clean cotton T-shirt. Always make sure to use a clean and washed cloth.

2. Never use a heating tray or put your kombucha next to any electromagnetic place because this way you can destroy the culture. So, in order to keep the heat between around 70° F and 85° F, try using a medium or a small heater. Make sure to keep it a few feet from your kombucha.

3. Never brew the kombucha in your closet!

Whenever you make kombucha, do not make the mistake of brewing it in your closet. Don't put the kombucha in a cabinet either or it will never grow because it won't be provided with the oxygen it needs to develop.

4. Don't add vinegar to the kombucha brew!

It is generally known that most people add a little quantity of apple cider vinegar to the first batch of kombucha, but you will surprised that you don't even need to use vinegar. If you wonder with what you can substitute for vinegar, use scoby and a tea as a starter.

5. Forgetting to stir your homemade kombucha tea.

It is possible that kombucha can be fizzy; if this happens to your brewed kombucha, don't panic; it can happen all the time because the yeast falls to the bottom of your container. To get rid of the problem of kombucha fuzziness, you have to strain it before starting a second round of fermentation. You will like the results after stirring the kombucha.

6. Don't oversteep your kombucha tea

When you add the black tea to the hot water, it releases the tannins together with other elements into the hot water. When you oversteep your kombucha tea, you may risk having a bitter taste and it can also weaken your scoby.

7. Don't rinse your scoby

Beginners and scoby brewers will think about rinsing their scoby when they add it to the tea. However, it is not compulsory to rinse the scoby and you should rather transfer it from one kombucha to another.

8. Don't use a bad quality scoby

The taste and the quality of your homemade kombucha are related to the health condition of the scoby itself. Check to see if your scoby is very thick, strong and healthy. It is recommended that the scoby you use should be thick as well as strong and rich in starter tea.

9. Don't store your kombucha in direct sunlight!

Brewing your homemade kombucha in the sunlight might harm it and weaken its culture. It is usually advised to avoid culturing your kombucha under the sunlight because the temperature outside is not constant and it can change which creates an unstable environment for the kombucha. So, you should brew any kombucha in a dark place like a cupboard.

10. Don't put the scoby in the refrigerator

Storing the scoby in the refrigerator can make it sensitive to a cold environment. In fact, excess cold can damage the microelements within the scoby and can weaken it. Over the time, your scoby will be weak and contaminated because of the mold and you will risk ruining the culture completely.

11. Don't cut sugar in your kombucha

You may think that you have added so much sugar to your kombucha and you will probably use less sugar, but this is not true. You should know that the primary effect of using sugar with kombucha is to feed your scoby and to help its fermentation. If you don't use enough sugar, the culture will not develop properly.

12. Don't add your scoby too soon to your liquid

Making your homemade kombucha needs patience and time. If you rush the process of fermenting and brewing your kombucha, you won't obtain the desired culture.

13. Don't use the wrong type of bowl!

If you commit a mistake and use an unsuitable bowl, you may risk obtaining a toxic kombucha tea. Use ceramic bowls or glass bowls.

14. Try not to use flavoured teas too much

It is always advised not to blend too many tea flavours in preparing kombucha, especially if you are making it for the first time.

15. Never use an aluminium pot to brew your homemade kombucha!

Don't prepare your sweet tea liquid in a pot made of aluminium because using it will harm the kombucha. So, you're better off avoiding using aluminium whenever you want a high-quality kombucha.

Chapter 11: Diverse Kombucha Frequently Asked Questions

Studies have proved that kombucha is very beneficial for the human body and to maintain a balance lifestyle. However, there is still a sense of mysteriousness that surrounds kombucha and there are many questions that we are looking for answers to about this drink. There are various things we can still discover and learn about kombucha beverages, and the following questions will help you understand better what kombucha is.

1. Do we find dairy products in kombucha?

Absolutely no; the composition of your homemade kombucha is completely organic because it is made of organic sugar, black tea, and also distilled water.

2. Can we be sure that kombucha is gluten free?

Yes, kombucha is free of any gluten components and if you have any doubt, you can ask the seller.

3. What should I do if my kombucha is too sour?

Don't panic if the taste of your kombucha is too sour; it doesn't mean that the taste is ruined, but that it was left for a long time to ferment. And the good news is that there is a solution for the sour taste. You can add fruit juice to adjust the taste or you can use the kombucha to dress salads.

4. What should I do if my scoby shows blue spots?

If your scoby shows blue spots, it means that mold has affected your kombucha and this is a serious issue that can never be dealt with. What you have to do in this case is to throw the scoby away and clean your container very well with vinegar and water; then start the process of fermenting kombucha all over again.

5. What can I do if my kombucha is too sweet and not fermenting?

If you made sure that you have already added sugar to your kombucha, but it is not showing any signs of fermentation, it means that you should be patient and set the kombucha to ferment for a longer time. There are also some other options you can try; you should consider adding more starter tea. The problem can also be resolved by using green, black, or white tea.

6. How much time will a kombucha culture last?

You might think that a kombucha culture cannot last for a long time, but you will be surprised that you can use the culture a few times. You can also compost your cultures or recycle it after a few months.

7. How do I make my kombucha taste like that of grocery stores?

There are many tricks we can use to make our kombucha taste like that sold at groceries. We can add some additives like ginger, juice, and fruits.

8. Can I make my kombucha without tea starters?

The answer is absolutely yes; you can replace tea starters with a type of distilled white vinegar. Tea starters can also be substituted by raw bottled kombucha tea that you can buy from stores.

9. How can I tell that my kombucha culture is developing in a good way?

There are many signs with which we can deduce that the kombucha beverage is developing in a good and smooth way, like the appearance of brown particles of yeast. The taste of a good fermented kombucha culture becomes similar to that of vinegar.

10. How can I raise the degree of carbonation of a kombucha beverage?

In order to increase the process of carbonation of a kombucha culture, you can place it in a bottle that is airtight.

11. Does kombucha contain any alcohol?

Kombucha beverages, like any other fermented foods, contains an amount of alcohol. And despite the fact that the alcohol in kombucha varies from one batch to another, it is generally known that the percentage of alcohol is really small.

12. For how long can I brew my kombucha tea or beverage?

You can brew any kombucha drink for a period that lasts from about 7 to 29 or thirty days according to your preference. Keep in mind that any prolonged brewing time can result in obtaining a less sugary drink. The temperature has an important role in the time kombucha culture takes to develop.

13. Why are kombucha cultures sold in a very dehydrated state?

We choose to sell dehydrated cultures so that it will be safe to transfer it from one place to another.

14. What is the most suitable temperature to brew kombucha?

Kombucha is known for thriving at temperatures of 72 to 85 degrees F. Be careful, if the temperature hits the roof of 90 degrees, it will kill your kombucha.

15. Have you ever asked yourself how much of a kombucha beverage you should drink?

It is highly advised to drink kombucha before eating anything in the morning and you can start with 5 to 9 oz twice a day. After drinking kombucha, you should drink a huge quantity of water so that you can flush out the toxins from the body.

16. Is kombucha beneficial to get rid of stomach viruses?

Drinking kombucha is very beneficial in case you have any digestive problems and it can help cure it, thanks to its high levels of probiotics.

17. Can I use lemon juice to flavour my kombucha drink?

Lemon juice is a great choice for making a homemade kombucha, especially because it helps produce carbonation when it is used in the method of double fermentation.

18. What are the flavours that I can add to my kombucha?

You can use fruits to flavour your kombucha like strawberries, mango, grapes, cherries and so on.

19. Is it normal to see foam on your homemade kombucha?

To see foam on your kombucha is great news indeed because it means that your scoby is growing, so there is no need for you to worry if you notice foam.

20. Does drinking kombucha have any side effects?

If you feel a strange headache after you drink kombucha beverages, don't panic, it is normal and it might be because you drank too much. Just try slowing down and drink kombucha in small quantities at first.

21. Can pregnant women drink kombucha?

Yes, only if you are used to drinking kombucha before pregnancy; but if you have never tasted kombucha, then it is not a good idea to drink it, especially during the first months of pregnancy.

The Major Side Effects of Kombucha

Each type of food and beverage has many benefits, but also many side effects and kombucha is no exception. Despite the fact that kombucha is healthy and safe for consumption, it has some side effects sometimes.

1. Kombucha contains a small amount of alcohol.

2. Kombucha contains a small amount of caffeine and although this is a good effect, it can be harmful to drink it in the evening.

3. Kombucha is characterised by its ability to affect the level of blood glucose, so it is advised not to drink it before any already planned surgery as it may affect it.

4. Do not drink a kombucha beverage if you have a weak immunity. It may increase the risk of infections and it can catalyse infections.

5. You should be extra careful when buying kombucha; you have to get it from a known resource.

6. Poisoning is a possible risk of consuming kombucha. A study has shown that brewing kombucha in a ceramic container can lead to the absorption of a toxic element called lead from the container. Kombucha poisoning has many symptoms that you can notice, so don't hesitate to call a doctor in case you suspect poisoning.

7. Kombucha can rarely damage your liver

A damaged liver is a known effect that can result from drinking a kombucha beverage. In some cases, drinking kombucha can lead to complete liver failure, but this is very rare. In some cases, drinking kombucha can lead to a jaundice status, which starts with a yellow color of the skin and then the eyes and the nails become yellow, too.

Conclusion

Many people tend to choose kombucha as their favorite tea ingredient because it is rich in the healthiest types of bacteria and thanks to the presence of probiotics. Kombucha is not only capable of helping the body in digestion, but it also has a wide variety of benefits that are only connected to its unpasteurized version. Nutritionists have always been curious about kombucha and the results they have found have been astonishing. Indeed, Kombucha has proven to be a cure for many ailments and a great source of probiotic ingredients.

And while some people claim that kombucha is harmful, scientific evidence has shown that kombucha has magical health benefits and many people have found it efficient in fighting cancer and preventing it. So what is the truth about kombucha, or the mother of mushroom being a miracle? If you are eager to find out the answer, all you have to do is to read this book.

THANKS FOR READING THIS BOOK

If you found this material very helpful, feel free to share it with your friends. You can also help others find it for me to encourage me to continue writing books you love reading.

***

Again, I really appreciate you taking the time to read my book.

Regards, Jason Goodfellow

Made in the USA
Las Vegas, NV
05 March 2021